The Further Selected Poems of K Morris

K Morris

Contents

Copyright Page	i
Acknowledgements	v
The Dead May Speak	1
Dog Bed	2
To a Departed Dog	3
Grief	4
Flowers in My Mum's Garden	5
Wind and Tree	6
In Memory Of	7
Churchyard Tree	8
I Walked Alone	9
February Snow	10
This Winter Sunshine	11
A Confession	12
This Rhyme is Out of Time	13
I Face My Darkening Window	14
Pick Your Fights Wisely My Friend	15
Past Time	16
A Bird on the Wing	17
Sparrows in a Tree	18
Winter Bird	19
An Eliot Poem	20
I Hear the Rain	21
Fine Rain	22
Under Nature's Great Roof	23
Nature's Glass	24
On a Chilly Winter's Night	25

Bird	26
Lonely Train	27
December Snow	28
Caught Between Cassandra and Pangloss	29
Lost Amidst Numberless Fallen Leaves	30
The Poet Sees	31
Euphemism	32
"You're a Joker," She Said	33
Art and Sin	34
In Lockdown	35
On the Isle of Lesbos	36
Sugar Babe	37
The Past	38
As I Go	39
A Most Helpful Young Lady Named Yvette	40
A Musical Young Lady Named White	41
When a Young Lady Dancing in a Field	42
When an Elderly Spinster Named Jean	43
When My Friend Whose Name is Katie	44
Whilst Climbing Up a Very Steep Hill	45
Whilst Walking Through a Place Known as Soho	46
Whilst Drunk on Very Strong Beer	47
When I Went on a Halloween Date	48
I Awoke from a Most Horrible Dream	49
Paul the Anarchist	50
When I Entered a Luxurious Hotel Room	51
There Was a Young Lady of Dover	52
My Friend Whose Name is Bess	53

Anthologised	54
Poets Should Stick Together	55
Bess's Dress	56
Feisty	57
Whilst Walking Through a Very Thick Mist	58
Miss Shakespeare	59
Whilst Visiting the Great Count Dracula	60
A Most Rakish Old Gentleman Known as Paul	61
I Once Knew a Drover from Dover	62
Silver Fox	63
There is Comfort in This Tree	64
Miss Flow	65
Miss Brown	66
On Glancing under My Large Double Bed	67
If You Hear a Wicked Rumour	68
With Sincere Apologies to Edward Lear	69
Contact and Social Media	73

Copyright ©2021 K Morris.

All rights reserved. This book or any portion thereof may not be reproduced or used in any manner whatsoever without the express written permission of the author, except for the use of brief quotations in a book review.

To contact the author, please email kmorrispoet@gmail.com or visit their website at https://kmorrispoet.com/

To my beloved guide dog Trigger, who died on 1 September 2020. You left a hole in my heart.

Acknowledgements

I would like to thank the following:

Dave Higgins for proof reading and formatting my manuscript (any remaining errors are entirely my own).

And Shanelle Webb for her administrative assistance in producing this collection and for taking the photograph which adorns the front cover.

The Dead May Speak

The dead may speak
Through the poet's art.
His readers may weep.
Yet some things run so deep,
They can not be expressed in art.

Dog Bed

The mark
Of your teeth is still there
On your old dog bed.
I walk in the park,
Where
The dead
Leaves lie.
Shadows on the Grass
Mistook for an old friend.
All things pass,
However much we pretend
Otherwise. You closed your eyes
And left your mark
Upon my heart.

To a Departed Dog

Sometimes I see
You in front of me,
Or imagine you at
My side. I
Go to pat
You under the table,
Where you so often sat.
I am not able.
You are not coming back.

Grief

We say
"Our grief
Will never cease."

But each day,
Slowly, grief
Ebbs away.

Bittersweet regret.
Sometimes we forget
And laugh:
For all must pass.

Flowers in My Mum's Garden

Flowers in my mum's garden
Bring to mind
A former time
When my grandfather grew roses.

I remember the scent
Of roses in his garden.
And my attempt
To make perfume.

In youth,
Few engage with age;
And the truth
That roses
Are gone so soon.

Wind and Tree

As I
Pass by
A tree,
I hear the wind
And ponder
On my mortality.
And wonder,
How many see
In wind and tree,
Their own mortality?

In Memory Of

A bench replete
With flowers
In winter's wood.
Hours
Incomplete
Marked by a stone
Clock with lost hands.

We go into the unknown
Wood.
But perhaps a bench may stand
To commemorate
Those who, of a late
Winter afternoon,
Think on nature's passing bloom.

Churchyard Tree

A tall tree
Arrested me
As I
Passed by
The churchyard yesterday.

When I
Go away,
The tree will stay.
And others will pass by;
And, perhaps, think as I.

I Walked Alone

I walked alone
Through the graveyard.
Then, on reaching home,
I pondered on lovers
And the dead.
The graveyard plot
Is cold,
Whilst love is hot.
Yet the dead
And lovers
Both have their bed,
Do they not?

February Snow

Walking through the churchyard snow,
I think
On those below.

Footprints in the February snow
Soon will go.
But ink
On a page
May still engage

Though the poet is gone,
His words live on.
Else they go,
As does winter's snow.

This Winter Sunshine

This winter sunshine.
This ticking clock.
Now I am here.
Then I am not.

A Confession

A confession
About my obsession
With clocks.
Their ticks
And tocks.
But all obsessions
Eventually stop.

This Rhyme is Out of Time

This rhyme
Is out of time
And I have not the will
To set it right
Tonight.

I am no sage,
Yet dream of a golden age
When clocks kept slow time
And to rhyme
Was thought the proper thing to do.
Perhaps this view
Is at least half true.

I Face My Darkening Window

I face my darkening window.
My curtain
Will shut out the night.
I know
Morning's light
Must come.
But who can be certain
That he
Will see
The sun?

Pick Your Fights Wisely, My Friend

Pick your fights wisely, my friend.
You may pretend
That you can stop the clock.
Of course, you may
The clock's hands stay;
Or mock time
In a rhyme.
But, in the end,
Your inner clock
Will stop,
My friend.

Past Time

A rhyme
Captures a moment in time,
Of joy or pain,
Which will never come again.

The poet may change
His original rhyme;
But past time
He can not change.

A Bird on the Wing

A bird on the wing
Is such a temporary thing.
Though, when it dies,
In poetry, it survives.

Sparrows in a Tree

A myriad sparrows singing
To me from a tree.
Their song
Bringing
Joy to girl and boy.

I know not how long
My song
May be.
But sparrows in a tree,
Sang to me.

Winter Bird

I heard a bird
Flap in winter's air.
He will fly,
I know not where.
While I
Shall go
In winter's snow.

Does he know
His journey's end?
And what of thee
And me,
My friend?

An Eliot Poem

An Eliot poem,
Mingled with birds,
Made me lose
All my words.

I Hear the Rain

I hear the rain again.
How it does pour
Over city street and moor.
When I go my way,
The rain will stay.
And others will remain,
Listening to the rain.

Fine Rain

I get wet
By this fine
Rain.
Yet
I do not regret
For the divine
Is in the rain.

I shall get wet
Again.
For when
Death does steal
Me away,
I regret
That I shall no longer feel
The joy of a rainy day.

Under Nature's Great Roof

Under nature's great roof,
I feel the truth
In wind and rain.

When I am gone,
I shall be one
With wind and rain.

Nature's Glass

Flowers on either side
Of the path.
I
Can not decide
Whether to laugh
Or cry.

Flowers live and die,
While I
Smile
And pass
By,
Seeing in nature's glass
You and I.

On a Chilly Winter's Night

On a chilly winter's night
The song of a bird
I heard,
As he sang to me
From a churchyard tree.
Such delight
And poignancy.
But that was in me.

Bird

Yesterday, in the early morning,
I heard you speak.
Just your bleak
Cry and I,
Ere the light was dawning.

I think on Macbeth
And the impending death
Of another year.
A bird often unheard
But forever near.

Lonely Train

I have no resistance
To the lonely train
Which calls
From the distance.
Nor to the rain
Which falls
In this dark park.

December Snow

A typical December day.
The sun has stopped
Away
And the temperature has dropped.

The forecasters say
There may
Be snow.

I well remember the December
Snow.
And playing on frozen pond.
But oh so long Ago!

And I shall grow
Old and remember December
Snow.

We count the cost
Once things are lost.
Whilst the foolish, wishing to sunbathe,
Pray for the coming heatwave.

Caught Between Cassandra and Pangloss

Caught, between Cassandra and Pangloss,
We know not what
To think. So drink
To the great Pangloss.
But, in our empty glass,
We find the Trojan lass.

Lost Amidst Numberless Fallen Leaves

Lost
Amidst numberless fallen leaves,
The poet sees
The cost
Of it all.

Nymphs play in autumn's sun.
Winter must come.
And the poet sees
Half-forgotten leaves
Whirled by passion's passing breeze.

The Poet Sees

The poet sees
Young women's feet
Stamp on autumn leaves;
And writes a rhyme
To fleeting time,
Who will defeat
All he sees.

Euphemism

His girlfriend
Brought him delight
For the night.
But did not comprehend
The meaning of euphemism.
They took a decision
To pretend...

"You're a Joker," She Said

"You're a joker," she said,
Doubling over in laughter.
"If you didn't laugh
You would cry,"
Said I.

And after,
I felt proud
That I can still engage
With a girl half my age
And make her laugh out loud.

I hear Prufrock's footman snicker.
The stage
Lights flicker
Ere the curtain does fall,
Covering all.

Art and Sin

He sees the mind behind
Those stilettos
And her so short clothes.

There is bliss
In her kiss
For him.

Seeing her heart,
He ponders on art;
And what is sin.

In Lockdown

In lockdown, poets rhyme;
While a girl's smile,
And her precious time,
Are bought online.

After the wine
And giggles and wriggles,
Men are left bereft;
And poets rhyme.

On the Isle of Lesbos

On the isle of Lesbos, its all Greek
To the men who seek
Fun, sun,
And sand.
But the Euro may command
A goddess's hand,
And cause her to smile
And speak
The tourist's language for a while.

Sugar Babe

She took her face
To the market place
And found therein
Much wealth through sin.
She practised love's art;
And her heart
Became as tin.

The Past

Perhaps one ought
Not to look back.
Yet I walk
That old familiar track.

I pass the flats
(Once a bustling, hustling pub)
And remember idle talk
Over Sunday grub.

Having passed the flats,
I retrace my tracks.
For one can not go back
To what is long since gone.

As I Go

As I go,
I make footprints in the snow.
The red postbox continues to stand,
A symbol of a vanishing land.

Footprints will go,
Covered by snow.
And this dear England of mine—
Is it all in my mind?

A Most Helpful Young Lady Named Yvette

A most helpful young lady named Yvette
Has a job in my local laundrette.
A kindly old friar
Lives in a dryer
Where he's dried by that helpful Yvette.

A Musical Young Lady Named White

A musical young lady named White
Likes to visit me at midnight.
I've often seen
Her fine tambourine
As we play together at midnight.

There Once Was a Turkey Called Paul

There once was a turkey called Paul
Who, not liking Christmas at all,
Escaped one snowy Christmas Eve
With a fox called Steve...
The rest I fail to recall.

When a Young Lady Dancing in a Field

When a young lady dancing in a field
Said "All men to my charms must yield",
I said, "That's all very well
But, dear madam, can you tell
Me how to reach that place called Sheffield?"

When an Elderly Spinster Named Jean

When an elderly spinster named Jean
Called me a wicked old libertine,
My new friend Miss Hocking
Said, "I've lost my stocking.
And, Jean, what is a libertine?"

When My Friend Whose Name is Katie

When my friend, whose name is Katie,
Said, "I want to discuss something weighty",
I said, "You're not fat,"
And she really liked that.
But I felt bad lying to Katie!

Whilst Climbing Up a Very Steep Hill

Whilst climbing up a very steep hill
I met with a girl named Jill.
When I said, "Where is Jack?",
She gave me such a whack
That I rolled back down that hill!

Whilst Walking Through a Place Known as Soho

Whilst walking through a place known as Soho,
I met a girl who you may know.
She wore but one spectacle
And is not that respectable.
And I often like to visit old Soho...

Whilst Drunk on Very Strong Beer

Whilst drunk on very strong beer,
I met the late Edward Lear.
When I said, "You are dead!",
He turned to me and said,
"Yes, but I fancied a beer!"

When I Went on a Halloween Date

When I went on a Halloween date
With a girl who calls herself Kate,
We stopped by a grave
Where I met with Dave,
Who shares that grave with Miss Kate!

I Awoke from a Most Horrible Dream

I awoke from a most horrible dream
On the day that's known as Halloween.
I rubbed my eyes
And, to my surprise,
Found the Devil had eaten the cream!

Paul the Anarchist

There once was an anarchist named Paul
Who said, "All governments they must fall!"
So he huffed and he puffed,
And he wrote lots of stuff.
And governments took no notice of Paul!

When I Entered a Luxurious Hotel Room

When I entered a luxurious hotel room
And savoured the sweet scent of perfume,
I said, "My dear,
What brings you here?"
She said, "This is my hotel room!"

There Was a Young Lady of Dover

There was a young lady of Dover
Who was fond of rolling in clover.
A cow called Lou
Gave her a chew,
So she left off rolling in clover!

My Friend Whose Name is Bess

My friend whose name is Bess
Wears stilettos and a short dress.
That priggish Miss Coral
Says, "That girl's immoral!"
And she's totally right about Bess!

Anthologised

When anthologised
The poet's work survives.
He dies.
But every pure thought
(And kink)
Is forever caught
In ink.
Therefore, I think
That the poet, most wise,
Ought to shrink
From being anthologised...

Poets Should Stick Together

A poet whose name is Heather
Said, "We poets should stick together."
I said, "That's true."
And with strong glue,
I stuck myself to poet Heather!

Bess's Dress

There once was a young lady named Bess
Who was well known for her special dress.
That wise old Miss Rose
Speaks of the Emperor's Clothes;
And Bess who wore a very special dress.

Feisty

A young man named Guy
Liked to make women cry.
But pretty Miss Pearl,
Being a feisty girl,
Poked Guy in the eye!

Whilst Walking Through a Very Thick Mist

Whilst walking through a very thick mist,
I met with my friend the anthologist.
He said "Take a look
At this fine poetry book."
But I couldn't see through the mist!

Miss Shakespeare

I know a girl called Miss Shakespeare
Who has pulled me many a beer.
The old barman, named Macbeth,
Bores us all to death.
And King Duncan is off his beer.

Whilst Visiting the Great Count Dracula

Whilst visiting the great Count Dracula
I said, "Your view is truly spectacular.
But your breath is quite foul
And those wolves they do howl!
I regret I must leave Castle Dracula!"

A Most Rakish Old Gentleman Known as Paul

A most rakish old gentleman known as Paul.
Said, "A happy new year to you all.
Especially all you young women
Who do nothing but sinning!"
He's a most dissolute old gentleman is Paul!

I Once Knew a Drover from Dover

I once knew a drover from Dover
Who knitted all his livestock a pullover.
A young lady walking by
Said, with a great sigh,
"Your livestock look daft in that pullover!"

Silver Fox

An elderly gentleman named Mr Box
Is known as the Silver Fox.
Whilst the young women say
My hair it is grey.
But I'm not rich like Box!

There is Comfort in This Tree

There is comfort in this tree
For it was here before me;
And will stay
When I am clay,
To comfort those who pass
Along this self-same path

A few, perhaps
Gazing at this tree,
May remember me.
I laugh
For a tree
Has no vanity.

Miss Flow

A young lady named Miss Flow
Has morals so extremely low
That a dissolute old rake
Jumped in a great lake
To escape that low Miss Flow!

Miss Brown

Last night, whilst out on the town,
I met a young lady named Brown.
Awaking in the early morning
With much stretching and yawning,
I found neither my wallet nor Brown!

On Glancing under My Large Double Bed

On glancing under my large double bed,
I found a young lady in red.
Her name it is Lou
And she's mislaid a shoe.
So I'm helping Lou under my bed.

If You Hear a Wicked Rumour

If you hear a wicked rumour
About an extremely beautiful young perfumer
By the name of Miss White
And what we did last night,
Remember she's a beautiful young perfumer!

With Sincere Apologies to Edward Lear

The owl and the pussycat went to sea in a leaky,
    cardboard boat.
They had lost all their money
To a girl called Honey,
Along with a £5 note.

The owl looked up to the stars above
And sang to a small guitar
"Oh beautiful pussy, oh pussy my love,
I wonder where we are?
We are? We are?
I wonder where we are?"

With a sorrowful sigh
The pussy made reply:
"Owl,
You are a stupid old fowl!
Make no mistake
We
Are not at sea
But on a lake!
Oh what a stupid old fowl you are,
You are,
You are!
Oh what a stupid old fowl you are!"

So they sailed away
For a year and a day
To the land where the bong tree grows.
And there in a wood
A stoned student stood
Blowing smoke from the end of his nose,
His nose,
His nose.
Blowing smoke from the end of his nose.

"Dear student, are you willing
To sell for one shilling
Your pot?" Said the student, "I will."
So they took it away
And were arrested next day
By the policeman who lives on the hill...

Contact and Social Media

To contact Kevin, please send an email to kmorrispoet@gmail.com.
Website: https://kmorrispoet.com/
Twitter: https://twitter.com/drewdog2060_
Instagram: https://www.instagram.com/kmorrispoet/
To sign up to Kevin's monthly author newsletter please follow this link: https://mailchi.mp/426d57064ebd/sign-up-to-my-newsletter

Printed in Great Britain
by Amazon